Connections Guide

to

John Steinbeck's

Of Mice and Men

by
Stephen Fender

Contents

NOTES

What does the title mean?

The phrase "Of Mice and Men" comes from a poem
by the Scottish romantic poet Robert Burns (1759
— 96), called "Tae a Moose" ["To a Mouse"].
Written in 1785, it is a farmer's address to a mouse
whose nest he has turned up with his plough. The
farmer apologises for breaking into the natural
cycle in which the mouse is preparing for winter:

> *I'm truly sorry man's dominion Has broken Nature's
> social union,*

but observes that

> *Mousie, thou art no thy lane [not alone],*
> *In proving foresight may be vain: The best-laid*
> *schemes o' mice an' men Gang aft a-gley [Go oft*
> *awry],*
> *An' lea'e us nought but grief an' pain, For promis'd*
> *joy!*

What happens in the story?

George and Lennie, two itinerant farm workers in
the 1920s, are on their way south to join the
workforce on a grain ranch near Soledad,
California. They are on the run from some trouble
they got into in Weed, at the far north of the state,
when the simple-minded Lennie tried to stroke a

girl's red dress, and was accused of rape. In the late afternoon, as they try to get to their new place of work, the bus driver leaves them off nearly four miles from the ranch, so they decide to bed down for the night by the Salinas river.

It soon becomes clear that George does the thinking for the two of them. Lennie is huge but mentally slow. He likes to pet small furry animals, and indeed is hiding a dead mouse in his pocket, having killed it by his over-attentive stroking. George throws it across the river.

As they prepare a supper of beans cooked in their cans over a fire, Lennie urges George to tell the story that soothes and pleases him whenever he hears it: how one day they are going to have their own house with a couple of acres and a cow and some pigs, a vegetable patch, some chickens and — this is what Lennie most likes to hear — rabbits for him to feed and pet.

The next day, when they turn up at the ranch, George tells Lennie to let him do the talking. Though the boss wonders about their relationship, George convinces him that Lennie is very strong, and that they will both work hard. After they are hired, Candy, the old caretaker who has lost one hand in a farm machine, invites them to select their beds in the bunkhouse. Curley, the aggressive son of the boss, comes in looking for his wife. Soon after Curley's wife visits the bunkhouse asking for her husband, George tells Lennie to have nothing to do with her.

Toward Los Angeles, California by Dorothea Lange

As the field hands come in for lunch, the new employees meet Slim, the tall jerkline skinner who drives the combine harvester, and Carlson, who totes the grain bags. Slim's bitch has just "slung" five pups. Carlson suggests he give one to Candy, whose old dog is nearly blind, and smells and is so lame that it can hardly walk.

The next day discussion returns to dogs old and new. Carlson persuades an unwilling Candy to let him shoot the old one, suggesting that he take one of Slim's new-born pups. Slim offers Lennie a pup too, though cautions him to leave it with its mother until weaned. Curley comes in again looking for his wife, then, hearing voices in the barn, rushes out thinking he'll find Slim and his wife together. Slim faces him down. Curley returns to the bunkhouse and, full of displaced anger, picks a fight with Lennie. Unwilling to fight, Lennie is eventually goaded to catch Curley's hand, then crush it until the bones are broken. The other men take Curley to Soledad for treatment, after warning him to say that he caught his hand in a machine, unless he wants his humiliating defeat to become common knowledge.

When Candy overhears George and Lennie talking about their little dream farm, he reveals that he has a sizeable stake saved up, which he offers to add to their much more meagre savings if they will let him join them. Since George already knows of a place going for what they can afford, it begins to look as though the dream may come true.

The next night is Saturday, when most of the men go off to the brothel in town — George just to drink. Left behind are Lennie, Candy and Crooks, the black stable hand. They meet in Crooks's room in the stable, where they are not normally invited by the lonely but proud inhabitant. Lennie and Candy tell Crooks about their plan to buy a farm with George. Crooks ridicules the idea, saying that he has seen hundreds of itinerant workers with the same dream – a dream that never comes true. But when he hears that they really have the money, he asks if can come along, doing odd jobs, not for a salary but for room and board alone.

Just then Curley's wife comes in. She admits to being lonely, and says she knows where the other men have gone. "They left all the weak ones here," she says. Lennie is entranced by her, but Candy tells her they don't want her there, and boasts of having "our own ranch house to go to". She mocks the idea. When she notices the bruises on Lennie's face she realises that Curley's hand is more likely to have been caught in Lennie's fist than in a machine.

The next day Lennie has taken his new puppy out of its mother's nest into the barn, in order to coddle it unobserved. The more he pets the little animal the harder his strokes get, until finally he breaks its neck. Curley's wife comes in. When she sees the dead puppy and notes Lennie's distress, she consoles him. "He was jus' a mutt," she says. She tells Lennie that she doesn't really like Curley, and says she could have gone to Hollywood to be in the movies. When Lennie confesses that he likes to pet soft things, she allows him to touch her hair. As his strokes get stronger and more urgent, she begins to scream and then to struggle. Terrified that George will discover that he "done a bad thing", Lennie tries to shut her up and hold her down, finally breaking her neck.

George has told Lennie that in case of trouble, or if they get separated, they should meet back at the river where they camped out that first night. So Lennie takes off for the river bank. When the others discover the body, Curley forms them into a lynching party. Carlson reveals that his pistol has been stolen, so Curley and the other ranch hands assume that Lennie has it. Knowing where to find Lennie, George heads for the river camp. When he arrives, Lennie is surprised that he's not angry. Instead George tells him the story once again of the now impossible dream of their little farm. As he encourages Lennie to look across the river and the sound gets louder of the others crashing through the undergrowth, George uses Carlson's pistol to shoot Lennie in the back of the head.

What made *Of Mice and Men* different?

Of Mice and Men came out in 1937, shortly after Steinbeck's *In Dubious Battle* and before his *The Grapes of Wrath*. *In Dubious Battle* was an ambitious attempt to analyse the struggles of California farm labour in the light of a dubious bio- psychological theory, developed by a friend of Steinbeck's, which held that men behave differently when in large groups, or phalanxes, than they do when alone or in small groups. The novel, like the theory, has not stood the test of time: the characters are two-dimensional, the authorial voice over-didactic and intrusive.

Of Mice and Men was something of a reaction to *In Dubious Battle*. It was a return to material that the author knew first-hand. He now wanted to create a "little novel", he wrote in his journal, for which he must "find the beauty" (a quality missing from *In Dubious Battle*) and that would avoid the cause-and-effect movement towards a pre-determined theoretical position that drove the preceding book. In fact, says the biographer, Jackson Benson, his first working title for the manuscript was "Something that Happened", in order to suggest an accident, and thus establish a "non-teleological approach" to his new work. In its quiet way, however, *Of Mice and Men* was also an experiment. As Steinbeck's novels began to sell, so did the chances of their being adapted into plays, or even films. He had already sold the film rights to an earlier novel, *Tortilla Flat* – they would be sold again before the movie finally came out in 1942, starring Hedy Lamarr and Spencer Tracy – and he was becoming interested in the process by which fiction is converted into a film script. Besides, he seemed to want to get away from the excessive authorial comment and sign-posting of *In Dubious Battle*.

The solution was to write a novel as much like a play as possible: a narrative made up largely of dialogue accompanied by only enough description to set the scene, and with no passages of editorialising. That's just what *Of Mice and Men* is: a "play-novelette", as one critic called it.

With its action conveyed mainly through its dialogue and with just four locations – the river bank, the bunkhouse, Crooks's room and the barn where Lennie kills Curley's wife – it was easily adapted for the theatre, so easily that a version was appearing on Broadway within a year of publication. Other adaptations followed, including a successful 1939 film with Lon Chaney Jr. as Lennie and Burgess Meredith as George.

From the start the book was a hit. It was taken up by the Book-of-the Month Club, which meant guaranteed sales of more than 350,000 even before the book came out. Critics praised the simple, unassuming realism of the new work. It is "not a 'proletarian novel' in the sense in which the arm-wavers currently use the term", said Joseph Henry Jackson in the San Francisco *Chronicle*, but rather a "simple story" about men "as human beings who think and do and desire the many and various things that men have always thought and done and longed for". "The theme is not, as the title would suggest, that the best laid plans of mice and men gang aft agley," said Fred T. Marsh in the *New York Times Book Review*, "but a play on the immemorial theme of what men live by besides bread alone. In sore, raucous, vulgar Americanism, Steinbeck has touched the quick in his little story."

An English critic, writing in the *Times Literary Supplement*, called the book "a small masterpiece" in the "tough-tender" school of American fiction. The reviewer for the London Mercury, however, was less generous: calling the final scene, in which George shoots Lennie to save him from being lynched, was "a triumph of the sentimental macabre" he said, while Dorothea Brande Collins, a New York critic – and wife of the self-styled fascist Seward Collins – wrote in the magazine edited by her husband that "surely no more sentimental wallowing ever passed for a novel, or had such a welcome, as this sad tale of a huge half-wit and his cowboy [sic] protector!" The reason why we might not notice the sentimentality, Brande Collins continued, is that "masculine sentimentality, particularly when it masquerades as toughness", is harder to spot than the feminine kind, but it can be recognised by "the romantic overestimation of the role of friendship, the wax-figure woman, bright, hard, treacherous, unreal... from whom it is a virtue to flee to masculine companionship" (American Review, April, 1937).

Though determined not to follow the liberal intelligentsia in liking the novel, Brande Collins did hit upon aspects of *Of Mice and Men* that even they would come to question once the dust had settled. In *On Native Grounds* (1942), his classic survey of modern American prose before World War II, the New York liberal Alfred Kazin would write of "the calculated sentimentality of *Of Mice and Men*", while Mark Spilka, writing in Modern Fiction Studies (Summer 1974), would follow Brande Collins's lead in connecting male sentimentality to the fearful vision of the predatory woman.

What sort of ranch is Steinbeck describing?

A common – indeed, virtually universal – misreading of the novel is that *Of Mice and Men* is about migrant farm workers.[*] The book is almost always written and talked about as one of Steinbeck's three novels about migrants in the Great Depression. Even Jackson Benson, Steinbeck's most authoritative biographer, refers to the author's "concern with migrant farm labor" that led him to "three of his greatest novels, *In Dubious Battle*, *Of Mice and Men*, and *The Grapes of Wrath*", and the three books are commonly referred to as Steinbeck's "Dust Bowl novels".

This is understandable. Not only did Steinbeck publish his work at the height of the Great Depression, in 1937, but his book foreshadows the suffering experienced by agricultural workers during it. In its story of broken dreams and a desperate hunt for work, it reflects the mood and atmosphere of America in the 1930s even if Steinbeck was in fact depicting a slightly earlier world, the world of the 1920s, and, for the details of the action, locale and characters drawing on his experience – during holidays from school and college – working on hay and grain ranches.

[*] A distinguished exception to this misconception is Anne Loftis's "A Historical Introduction to *Of Mice and Men*", in Jackson Benson, ed., The Shorter Novels of John Steinbeck

Surprisingly, perhaps (given the degree to which the novel is associated with the Depression), this comes out vividly in the 1992 film of the novel, directed by Gary Sinise and starring John Malkovitch. According to the *New York Times,* the 1992 film "remains faithful in almost every way to the stark Steinbeck tale" – more so than the darker, more melodramatic 1940 film – and "emphasizes something in the original work that never before seemed of foremost importance: *Of Mice and Men* is a mournful, distantly heard lament for the loss of American innocence. This has always been in the Steinbeck novella, but it is the dominant mood of the film."

But for all that, if we are properly to understand *Of Mice and Men* it is essential to grasp that the novel is set before the Depression, in the 1920s, not in the 1930s. George and Lennie are not from out of state; they are native-born Californians. They are not migrants; they are itinerants. Unlike the Joads in *The Grapes of Wrath*, they are not a family; they are lonely individuals. They never had their own small farm to lose and leave, though they dream vainly of having one in the future.

Another difference between the 1920s and 1930s was the farm labour situation. In the depression of the 1930s, the families driven off their mid-western farms by hostile nature and economics flooded into California. With the supply of labour vastly exceeding demand for it, wages plummeted – that is, if there were any jobs at all. In *Of Mice and Men*, though, there is no suggestion that jobs are hard to come by, or wages depressed. George and Lennie get a job on the grain ranch through an employment agency in San Francisco, and the job is there waiting for them when they arrive. If their employment is, or has been, precarious, it's not because there are too many workers chasing the jobs available, but because of Lennie's love of heavy petting.

For the details of the novel's action, locale and characters Steinbeck drew on his experience – during holidays from school and college – working on hay and grain ranches. Unlike the migrants in the two novels set in the 1930s, the workers in *Of Mice and Men* are not picking apples, peaches, grapes or cotton, or any other orchard or row crop. They are harvesting grain, and grain was harvested by machines, not men. In the 1920s combine harvesters were huge contraptions with a "header" mounted alongside, consisting of a powered cutting edge called a sickle-bar, and a conveyor belt to carry the cut grain into the machine. Then, on board the machine, a series of fans, belts, screens and shaking sieves worked to separate the grain from the stem and blow the chaff out the back. All this machinery was motivated through gears and belts by one of the wheels on which the whole thing rolled, a steel driving wheel with deep flanges around its rim, to prevent it from skidding.

An early twentieth-century combine harvester, pulled by horses

So the tractive effort needed to pull the combine harvester over the field was more than required just to tow a large, heavy vehicle; it had to be strong enough also to turn the wheel that worked the machinery required for the whole job of cutting and winnowing the grain. By the 1930s tractors began to pull harvesters, and the machinery was driven by on-board engines. But in the 1920s both the machinery and the movement of the harvester required the power of teams of horses, or more commonly mules, lots of them – from 20 to 32 in a train, or even more. (Indeed the nature of the combine harvesters in *Of Mice and Men* is another reminder that this is a novel set in the 1920s, not the 1930s.)

The crew needed to run the harvester would include a header tender to guide the cutting edge

up and down to follow the contours of the field –
so that it didn't ride too high over the top of the
grain heads or, alternatively, run itself into the
ground – and two men to manage the burlap sacks,
catch the grain, sew up the tops of the sacks when
they were full, then throw them off the back. At
least two more men would be needed to heft the
sacks on to a flat bed truck or trailer to carry them
to the barn, or wherever the grain was to be stored.

What do the characters in *Of Mice and Men* actually do?

Slim is the

> *jerkline skinner, the prince of the ranch, capable of
> driving ten, sixteen, even twenty mules with a single
> line to the leaders. He was capable of killing a fly on
> the wheeler's butt* with a bull whip without touching
> the mule.*

George may know how to sew sacks, but it's more
likely that he, and certainly Lennie, will just be
humping them. When quizzed by the Boss, George
claims all sorts of skills for Lennie, but it's clear

---

*   That is, the rear end of the animal nearest the machine.

he's going to "rassel grain-bags", that he is mainly good for his strength: "He can put up a four-hundred-pound bale," as George tells the Boss. And later Slim confirms Lennie's strength: "I never seen such a worker," he says to George. "He damn near killed his partner buckin' barley'." Whit is another bag rasseler, as his introduction hints: "A young laboring man...his shoulders...bent forward...as though he carried the invisible grain bag."

As for the supporting help, Candy is the swamper, who sweeps and mops out the bunkhouse and sets out wash bowls and towels for the field hands when they come in from work. He gets his job title not from an association with water, but from the world of the southern states in the mid 1850s, when an assistant who cleared the roads to allow logging in the swamps was known as a swamper. Later the term came to mean a handyman, or an unskilled assistant to a skilled worker.

Crooks is the stable buck. "Buck" could be slang either for his rank (as in "buck private", the lowest rank in the army) or his colour. He feeds the animals and looks after the harnesses, keeping them clean and in repair.

The ranch personnel form a pecking order, or rather two pecking orders: one natural and one artificial. Slim is at the top of the natural hierarchy. He is taller than the other men. They defer to him in all kinds of ways, even letting him go first through the bunkhouse door, as Carlson does when they are about to have dinner. On his initial appearance Slim is described as moving "with a majesty only achieved by royalty and master craftsmen". At the bottom of the natural scale are those disabled by injury, like Candy, who has lost his hand in an accident, and Crooks with his bad back – further disadvantaged by his colour.

The artificial hierarchy is the one that counts when it comes to the political economy — the power to hire and fire the farm hands. At the top is the boss. Further down comes Curley, largely lacking in natural authority but retaining plenty of the other kind because he is the boss's son. His high-heeled cowboy boots brand him as a vain poseur with no useful role on a grain ranch. The fact that he wears a glove filled with Vaseline to keep his right hand soft for his wife suggests a cautious, even panicky possessiveness, and is a further index of his vanity, since he does no manual labour to make his hands hard in the first place. Curley's wife is something of a wild card: the men fear her because they think that any contact with her will get them into trouble with Curley, but it's not clear whose side she would take in a crisis, especially after Lennie crushes Curley's hand, thus demoting him in both natural and artificial hierarchies.

What is the relationship between George and Lennie?

From the boss on down, the way the ranch hands react to the partnership of George and Lennie tells the reader a lot about their social environment, not to mention their human sympathies. Except for Slim, the hands are suspicious, if not downright hostile. The boss suspects George of exploiting Lennie, maybe even living off his earnings. When Lennie panics at the boss's questions and George answers for him, the boss says "Say – what you sellin'?...what stake you got in this guy? You takin' his pay away from him?"

Curley assumes they're gay. When George explains – "We travel together" – he sneers: "Oh, so it's that way." Even Slim wonders about their relationship:

> *"Funny how you and him string along together." It was Slim's confident invitation to confidence.*
>
> *"What's funny about it?" George demanded defensively.*
>
> *"Oh, I dunno. Hardly none of the guys ever travel together. You know how the hands are, they just come in and get their bunk and work a month, and then they quit and go out alone. Never seem to give a damn about nobody."*

George admits that he used to bait Lennie, "but he was too dumb even to know he had a joke played on him. I had fun. Made me seem God damn smart alongside of him." In time, though, it wasn't so much fun, not least because Lennie was too stupid to get mad. But Slim offers the alternative suggestion that Lennie is too good natured to retaliate: "'He's a nice fella,' said Slim. 'Guy don't need no sense to be a nice fella... Take a real smart guy and he ain't hardly ever a nice fella.'"

In fact the friendship is a little like a marriage. The first time George retells the paradisal story about their little dream farm, he comments that other farm workers "don't belong no place", and because they "blow their stake" they "ain't got nothing to look ahead to". But with the two of them it's different. "We got a future. We got somebody to talk to that gives a damn about us... If them other guys goes in jail they can rot for all anybody gives a damn. But not us."

> Lennie broke in. "But not us! An' why? Because... because I got you to look after me, and you got me to look after you, and that's why." He laughed delightedly. "Go on now George."
> "You got it by heart. You can do it yourself."

But the relationship is fraught with tension. When Lennie asks for ketchup for their beans, George explodes:

*"Well we ain't got any... Whatever we ain't got,
that's what you want. God a'mighty, if I was alone I
could live so easily. I could get a job an' work, an' no
trouble... An' whatta I got?... I got you! You can't
keep a job an' you lose me ever' job I get... An' that
ain't the worst. You get in trouble. You do bad
things, an' I got to get you out... You crazy son- of-a-
bitch. You keep me in hot water all the time."*

To keep these resentments at bay, George issues
simple commands to Lennie to keep him out of
trouble. As he says to Slim, "Jus tell Lennie what
to do an' he'll do it if it don't take no figuring. He
can't think of nothing to do himself, but he sure
can take orders."

But occasionally these orders get more
complicated, if not contradictory, as when George,
referring to Curley, says to Lenny: "Don't let him
pull you in [to a fight] – but if the son-of- a-bitch
socks you – let 'im have it":

"Let him have what, George?"
"Never mind, never mind. I'll tell you when."

Later, with Curley looking for trouble, George
warns: "If there's any fightin', Lennie, you keep out
of it". Lennie agrees: "I don't want no fight."

Yet when Curley can't intimidate Slim or even
Carlson or Candy, he turns on Lennie, slashing
with his left, then smashing his nose with his right,
making it bleed profusely. Lennie is terrified, tries

to back away, and pleads: "'Make 'um let me alone, George'... too frightened to defend himself." At this point George jumps to his feet, yelling for Lennie to "Get him... Don't let him do it." Then, when Slim offers to get Curley himself, George repeats the order: "Get 'im, Lennie!" and then again: "I said get him." It's only when Lennie catches one of Curley's hands and starts to crush it that George tells him to stop. By then it's too late; George has to slap Lennie's face again and again until "Suddenly Lennie let go his hold. He crouched cowering against the wall. 'You tol' me to, George,' he said miserably."

As indeed he did. After they first meet Curley, George confides: "Ya know, Lennie. I'm scared I'm gonna tangle with that bastard myself. I hate his guts. Jesus Christ!" So for all his fear that Lennie will do more "bad things", get them into trouble and lose them yet another job, he's willing to use Lennie to enact a violent assault he dare not attempt himself.

So Mark Spilka is right to comment that for all his patient care of Lennie, "George himself invites the troubles ahead, makes things go astray, uses Lennie to provoke and settle his own quarrel with a hostile world."

*   Mark Spilka, "Of George and Lennie and Curley's wife," in Benson, ed., *The Short Novels of John Steinbeck*.

What's eating Curley's wife?

Curley's wife is a female stereotype. Throughout the novel she is made to act the role of what Dorothea Brande Collins called "the wax-figure woman, bright, hard, treacherous, unreal...from whom it is a virtue to flee to masculine companionship". Even before she appears, Candy tells George that she's been giving Slim and Carlson the eye, that he thinks "Curley's married...a tart". When George first meets her, he falls right into Candy's prejudice: "Jesus, what a tramp." Her red nails, the rouge of her "full" lips, her red mules, all remind him of the girl in Weed, no doubt, whose red dress so attracted Lennie and got him accused of rape, but they also associate her with the Whore of Babylon in the Book of Revelations, "arrayed in purple and scarlet colour, and decked with gold and precious stones and pearls, having a golden cup in her hand full of abominations and filthiness of her fornication".

Lennie is smitten: "She's purty," he says. This prompts a furious reaction from George:

> Listen to me, you crazy bastard," he said fiercely. "Don't you even take a look at that bitch. I don't care what she says and what she does. I seen 'em poison before, but I never seen no piece of jail bait worse than her. You leave her be."

When it comes to sex, George is, to put it mildly, on the defensive. Though he'll "have a shot" – that is, take a drink – at "Suzy's place", he won't go in for the full service, because "Me an Lennie's rollin' up a stake". Still he prefers a visit to a brothel to any encounter with an ordinary woman:

> George sighed. "You give me a good whore-house every time," he said."A guy can go in an' get drunk an' get ever'thing outa his system all at once an' no messes. An' he knows how much it's gonna set him back. These here jail baits is just set on the trigger of the hoosegow."

This is very odd: "jail bait" is an expression for a woman, sexual relations with whom would land you in jail, or the "hoosegow". Commonly this meant sex with someone under 18, the age of consent in California then and now. To be more precise, it meant statutory rape. Much less commonly – and this seems to be the sense in which George is using the phrase – it referred to actual rape, the rape of an adult woman by a man. What George seems to fear, in other words, is that Curley's wife might entice someone like Lennie into a sexual approach, only to accuse him of rape. Something of this sort seems to have happened in Weed. And also to Andy, whoever he is: "'Andy's in San Quentin right now on account of a tart,' said George."

Yet when George tells Slim what happened in Weed, he describes the incident as the result of fear and incomprehension *on both sides*, rather than a malign subterfuge on the woman's part. It's possible that some mature women lurk about to entice sexual advances from men whom they can accuse of rape, and get sent to jail, but how many and why? What would be the inducements, unless the men were rich, which George and Lennie are not? But for George, all women are "jail bait", apart from whores.

In other words, if feminists were boxers, the character of Curley's wife would be Steinbeck leading with his chin. In her Student Companion to John Steinbeck, Cynthia Burkhead recites the feminist indictment of the character. First, she has no name, not only inviting less of the reader's sympathy, but also throwing herself open to being read as a representative of women generally. She is presented as a whore with the evil eye. She is seen as a corrupting force in the male environment of the novel, "always moving about where she is not supposed to be, always searching for her husband, ostensibly, in the male territories of the bunkhouse and the barn". Only in death is she rendered harmless, even beautiful, with a face that is "sweet and young". This treatment by Steinbeck, Burkhead concludes, contributes to the prejudice against women that results in the consideration of women as "other".

Mark Spilka assumes that this hostility towards Curley's wife arises from some trauma in Steinbeck's early life. Recalling that *Of Mice and*

The original poster for Lewis Milestone's 1939 film Of Mice and Men

Men arises from the author's "boyhood summers" spent working on a grain ranch, Spilka suggests that the young Steinbeck might have been disturbed by "the masculine grossness and insecurity of the bunkhouse", the "whorehouse visits and combative marriages like Curley's".

FIVE FACTS ABOUT JOHN STEINBECK AND *OF MICE AND MEN*

1.

In the 1930s, Steinbeck was a member of The League of American Writers, a communist organisation for writers and critics.

2.

Of Mice and Men still appears on the American Library Association's Top 100 Banned Books; it ranked fifth on the list between 2000-2009.

3.

Steinbeck's criticisms of the US government apparently led to J. Edgar Hoover ordering the IRS (America's tax authority) to audit Steinbeck's taxes every year, just to annoy him.

4.

The 1939 film adaptation of *Of Mice and Men* was nominated for four Oscars.

5.

Steinbeck may have been a spy during the Cold War. CIA records released in 2012 show Steinbeck offered his services, which the agency was keen to take up. It is still not known what role, if any, Steinbeck played.

How fair is feminist criticism of the novel?

When the director George Kaufman read Of Mice and Men with the idea of turning it into the Broadway production, he wrote to Steinbeck to say that the novel "drops almost naturally into play form", but wondered whether Curley's wife "could be drawn more fully", since "she is the motivating force of the whole thing and should loom larger".[*]

So Steinbeck added a few speeches to the role of Curley's wife in the play script, the most substantial of which comes in the final barn scene. Lennie isn't listening, still preoccupied with the dead puppy, but Curley's wife reveals that her father, a sign-painter when he was working and wasn't blind drunk, tried to run away with her after a terrible row with her mother:

> *"I was pretty sleepy. He picked me us an' he carried me on his back. He says, 'We gonna live together because you're my own little girl an' not no stranger. No arguin' and fightin',' he says, 'because you're my little daughter.' (Her voice becomes soft.) He says, 'Why, you'll bake little cakes for me, an' I'll paint pretty pitchers all over the wall.' (Sadly) In the morning they caught us...wan' they put him away. (Pause.) I wish we'd 'a' went."*

[*] George F. Kaufman, quoted in Steinbeck: A Life in Letters.

But Steinbeck had much more to add in a remarkable letter to Claire Luce, who played Curley's wife on Broadway. Apparently the actress, despite rave reviews for her performance in a production which played to packed houses, began to have misgivings about the character's motivation. Prompted by a mutual friend, Steinbeck wrote to her about how he'd imagined Curley's wife's back-story.

> *She grew up in an atmosphere of fighting and suspicion. Quite early she learned that she must never trust any one...She was told over and over that she must remain a virgin because that was the only way she could get a husband... She is a nice, kind girl and not a floozy. No man has ever considered her as anything except a girl to try to make... As to her actual sexual life – she has had none except with Curley and there has probably been no consummation there since Curley would not consider her gratification and would probably be suspicious if she had any.* *

These don't seem to be the words of a misogynist, let alone one who constructs women as "the other". On the contrary, they show an understanding of women far beyond the

---

*   John Steinbeck to Claire Luce, Los Gatos [1938], in *Steinbeck: A Life in Letters*: "consummation" is almost certainly Steinbeck's word for orgasm, a necessary euphemism before the era of franker discussions of women's sexuality.

comprehension of the men in *Of Mice and Men*, and pinpoint the source of Curley's anger and aggression with a high degree of accuracy.

Cynthia Burkhead says that "a feminist reader is not interested in authorial intent. Whatever the author may have hoped to convey is irrelevant in comparison to what is actually presented in the text."

But what Burkhead and others fail to recognise is the dramatic nature of the novel, not to mention the play – that there is a deliberate, artistically constructed distance, in other words, between the mental and moral world of the author and his characters. It is Curley, Candy, George and the other men who have this complex problem with women, not John Steinbeck, and the coherence and consistency of the dramatic environment is down to Steinbeck's imaginative creativity, not to a defect in his own mindset.

Just how carefully the moral and behavioural environment of the ranch hands has been constructed can be seen in the matter of their names. Much has been made, by Burkhead, Spilka and many others, of the fact that Curley's wife has no name. But very few of these people are known by their given names. Slim is called Slim because he is slender, Curley has curly hair, Crooks's bad back has made him stoop. Lennie's surname is Small – real enough but picked up in the text as an ironic nickname, like "Tiny" for a big fat man. The boss isn't given a name either; so the absence of a name for Curley's wife is not so unusual in this social environment.

The crucial literary method in *Of Mice and Men* is to tell the story, and mediate the relationships between characters, from the point of view of the ranch hands themselves, not through an overbearing authorial narrative. And the reason these characters aren't interested in names – beyond simple designation of function and role – is that their insecurity discourages close personal affections. They are not members of a family; they are a collection of itinerant workers on temporary contracts: some just passing through, like Lennie and George, some more permanent (to the point of virtual imprisonment, in the case of Crooks and Candy), but none with employment rights – let alone benefits like pensions and medical care – that would tie them emotionally or financially to their employers. A skilled worker like Slim might be secure in his job (at least until 20-mule trains are replaced by caterpillar tractors), but the others are always liable to be "canned" or discarded as soon as they offend someone in power, or – like Candy's old dog – cease to be fit or useful. Their very mobility forces them to push close personal relationships to the background, or blank them out altogether.

So what is *Of Mice and Men* really about?

For six days a week from 1935 to 1962, Eleanor Roosevelt wrote a newspaper column called "My Day", in which she would apply her progressive vision to current events and larger issues, like race, the rights of workers and the place of women. Her column for 16 March, 1937, took as its topic the popular new book just out, *Of Mice and Men*. She called it "a marvellous picture of the tragedy of loneliness", and went on to reflect "how fortunate we are when we have real friends, people we can count on and turn to and who we know are always glad to see us when we are lonely".[*]

Literary critics even then might have considered this simple extraction of a novel's theme somewhat naive, yet the First Lady got straight to the heart of the book. *Of Mice and Men* is indeed about "the tragedy of loneliness".

This is why it is so important to recognise that the novel concerns itinerant rather than migrant farm workers. Migrants had families – *were* families, *worked* as families. So the threat to them was not loneliness but dissolution. In Steinbeck's *The Grapes of Wrath* (1939) the Joad family starts out from Oklahoma with Granma and Granpa, Ma

---

[*] Eleanor Roosevelt, "My Day," *New York World Telegram*, 16 March, 1937.

and Pa, their offspring – Tom, his older brother Noah, Al, his younger brother, Rose of Sharon and her husband Connie, Ruthie, the younger Joad daughter, and Winfield, the youngest Joad – not to mention Pa's older brother Uncle John. And that's just the family. Also along for the ride is the preacher Jim Casey.

Of these, first Granpa and then Granma die along the way, Noah, Connie and Casey defect, Tom has to go into hiding in California. Finally Rose of Sharon's baby is stillborn cutting the Joads off even from the next generation.

In *Of Mice and Men*, by contrast, the characters start out lonely, always have been, and always will be. The nearest town is Soledad, Spanish for "lonely place". It's a real place, but obviously chosen for its name. George is always playing solitaire, the American name for patience.

Even before they get to the ranch, George tells Lennie: "Guys like us, that work on ranches, are the loneliest guys in the world. They got no family. They don't belong no place."

As a result, they keep their emotional distance. Before they get to know each other, Candy says to George: "A guy on a ranch don't never listen nor he don't ast no questions."

Slim, as normative a voice as there is in the novel, confirms this view; he finds the companionship between George and Lennie unusual: "You know how the hands are, they just come in and get their bunk and work a month, and then they quit and go out alone. Never seem to give a damn about nobody." At times this distance suggests a more widespread alienation. Slim again: "Ain't many guys travel around together... I don't know why. Maybe ever'body in the whole damn world is scared of each other."

George "ain't got no people" and Candy "ain't got no relatives nor nothin". Of course, from Candy's point of view, his lack of family attachment makes the financing of their dream farm more straightforward, but generally the effect of solitude on the characters' morale is corrosive. Crooks, existentially lonely on account of his colour, explains the demoralising condition most explicitly:

> "S'pose you didn't have nobody. S'pose you couldn't go into the bunk-house and play rummy 'cause you was black. How'd you like that? S'pose you had to sit out here an' read books. Sure you could play horseshoes till it got dark, but then you got to read books. Books ain't no good. A guy needs somebody — to be near him... A guy goes nuts if he ain't got nobody. Don't make no difference who the guy is, long's he's with you. I tell ya," he cried, "I tell ya a guy gets too lonely an' he gets sick."

Related to their sense of isolation is the ranch hands' vulnerability to the labour market. They know they'll get the sack just as soon as they become useless. As Candy says: "I got hurt four years ago...They'll can me purty soon. Jus' as soon as I can't swamp out no bunk houses they'll put me on the county...You seen what they done to my dog tonight?"

If *Of Mice and Men* were a different kind of 1930s novel, this would be the point at which some union organiser would explain the benefits of labour solidarity. Lacking an extended family, these men could at least enjoy the fellowship and mutual support of their fellow workers.

But in *Of Mice and Men* the remedy offered is ownership of private property, the dream of that little two-acre farm. It's Crooks who makes that link explicit between solitude and the lack of land: "I seen guys nearly crazy with loneliness for land," he says, before offering himself as a willing, hard-working partner.

And in fact George's, Lennie's, Candy's (and now Crooks's) dream of the little farm is partly motivated by a need to stop being lonely. Their little house and farm entail co-operative working and companionship. And self-sufficiency, as George projects the vision:

"We'd jus' live there. We'd belong there. There wouldn't be no more runnin' round the country and gettin' fed by a Jap cook. No, sir, we'd have our own place where we belonged and not sleep in no bunk-house."

But the little farm will also guarantee their immunity from labour exploitation. As George says: "An' it'd be our own, an' nobody could can us."

But the story is only a fantasy. Candy bitterly, and unfairly, blames Curley's wife for spoiling the plan – "You God Damn tramp...you done it, didn't you? I s'pose you're glad" – but everything has conspired against it: their poverty, their precarious employment, their solitary condition, Lennie's unpredictable behaviour. As George says "softly":

"I think I knowed from the very first. I think I knowed we'd never do her. He usta like to hear about it so much I got to thinking maybe we would...I'll work my month an' I'll take my fifty bucks an' I'll stay all night in some lousy cat- house. Or I'll set in some pool-room till ever'body goes home. An' then I'll come back an' work another month an' I'll have fifty bucks more."

Is *Of Mice and Men* too pessimistic?

Interviewed by the *New York Times* around the time the play appeared on Broadway, Steinbeck related something of his experience that lay behind *Of Mice and Men*:

I was a bindle-stiff [tramp or itinerant worker] myself for quite a spell. I worked in the same country that the story is laid in. The characters are composites to a certain extent. Lennie was a real person. He's in an insane asylum in California right now. I worked alongside him for many weeks. He didn't kill a girl. He killed a ranch foreman. Got sore because the boss had fired his pal and stuck a pitchfork right through his stomach. I hate to tell you how many times. I saw him do it. We couldn't stop him until it was too late.[*]

It's interesting to compare this sequence of real-life events – real, that is, at least as remembered by the author – with what goes on in the book.

The real-life Lennie, angry that the boss fired his friend, attacked the perpetrator of the grievance – obviously an extreme, violent reaction, not to be emulated, but at least a logical response to the provocation. By contrast, the fictional Lennie kills an innocent victim, towards whom he feels no hostility, without motive, apart from a compulsion to stroke her hair. Notwithstanding his strength, it's hard to see how the sequence of action moves logically from stroking to neck-breaking.

The two Lennies also differ in their punishment. The "real" one, being thought unfit to plead, was not tried, let alone executed for murder, but was instead sent to an insane asylum. Lennie in the novel isn't so lucky. His crime, though

[*] 'Mice, Men and Mr. Steinbeck'. *New York Times*, Dec. 5, 1937.

completely unintended, is dealt with outside the law, by a lynching party hastily organised by a crazed husband who hated and feared his dead wife as much as he wanted her.

Against these odds, what are Lennie's chances?

Not good, but even so, did George have to shoot him? The authorial voice, expressed through Slim, that most normative of characters, says yes. "You hadda, George," Slim comforts the other man. "I swear you hadda." And he leads George away for a drink. The unspoken consensus seems to be that Lennie's mental disability, however it may have exonerated him from blame, would also render any incarceration intolerable.

So it's thought best to put him – and, let's face it, George – out of his misery. His killing was a mercy.

But how do we know that Lennie would feel better dead than locked up? It's hard to avoid the suspicion that another "logic" is operating in *Of Mice and Men*, one not related to ordinary cause and effect, but instead to something like fate.

Steinbeck's work was much indebted to the California literary naturalists like Frank Norris and Jack London, novelists preoccupied with the struggle between civilisation and natural forces. Norris's *McTeague* (1899) dramatises the tension between his protagonist's animal instincts and his limited rational control. London's *The Call of the Wild* (1903) is the tale of a domesticated and somewhat pampered dog kidnapped in California and taken to Alaska, where harsh treatment and a hostile natural environment cause him to discover his primal instincts in order to fight and survive.

Steinbeck's fellow novelist F. Scott Fitzgerald thought Steinbeck's debt to Frank Norris verged on plagiarism.* They certainly shared the theme of nature's power to override the "best laid plans" and hence the conviction that unless a story doesn't turn out for the worst it somehow isn't true. So McTeague dies of thirst and hunger and exposure in the desert handcuffed to his rival and pursuer, and Lennie in the book, unlike Lennie in real life, gets a bullet in the brain instead of due process and the asylum. So which outcome is more true?

THE LIFE AND TIMES OF
JOHN STEINBECK

Steinbeck was born in Salinas, California, in 1902. Salinas is just over 100 miles south of San Francisco, and about 20 miles inland from Monterey on the Pacific coast. From his time to the present day Salinas has been the county seat of Monterey County, and the hub of a thriving farming industry.

John was the third of four children of John Ernst Steinbeck, son of a German immigrant from North Rhine-Westphalia, and Olive Hamilton, who had been a schoolteacher before she married. They lived in a spacious Victorian house, still preserved in the town. After his father lost his job as manager for Sperry Flour, he opened a feed and grain store. When this failed, a close friend who managed the huge Spreckels Sugar refinery around two miles south of town took him on as a book-keeper. Later he settled as treasurer of Monterey County.

Like many writers, Steinbeck was captivated early by language. On his ninth birthday he was given a copy of Malory's *Le Morte d'Arthur*, revelling particularly in the old and obsolete words in the text. While in high school he used to stay up late at night writing stories and sketches, in an attempt to hone his descriptive skills.

In 1919 he went to Stanford University, 75 miles north in Palo Alto, where he studied on and off for six years, accumulating only three quarters of the units necessary for graduation. But, as an English major, he had the chance to read and write essays on literature. Above all he was able to attend a class on the short story taught by the legendary creative writing teacher Edith Mirrielees. She was the first qualified literary judge to spot Steinbeck's talent and to encourage his writing.

In between studies Steinbeck sought experience in travel and work. One of his earliest jobs, thanks to his father's connections, was on a barley ranch owned by the Spreckels Sugar Company. It was this early experience on which he drew for *Of Mice and Men*.

On leaving Stanford in 1925 Steinbeck worked at other odd jobs, then went to New York, where he spent a miserable six months trying and failing to get his short studies published. It was here that he started his first full-length work of fiction, *Cup of Gold*, "A Lusty Buccaneer Novel" (as the blurb on the paperback reprint would have it), based on the life of the 17th century privateer Henry Morgan.

Returning to California, broke and dispirited, he got a job as a caretaker in the large house of a friend in Lake Tahoe, the resort in the California Sierra Nevada mountains. Off season, he remained in a cabin in the grounds, finishing *Cup of Gold*. He also worked as a tour guide at a trout hatchery in nearby Tahoe City, where he met his first wife, Carol Henning, who was up from San Francisco on vacation.

The couple moved, first to Los Angeles, then to Pacific Grove on the Monterey Peninsula, living in a cottage owned by his father. Supported by free housing, loans from his father and the additional gift of all the manuscript paper he could use, Steinbeck began to write furiously. *Cop of Gold* (1929) had been a flop so he decided to do something more immediate, local and contemporary – always a smart move for him. The result was *The Pastures of Heaven* (1932), a collection of short stories loosely based on the country inhabitants of the Corral de Tierra, a beautiful valley in Monterey County.

Now determined to embark on something more ambitious, he produced a strenuous family saga called *To a God Unknown* (1933) about settlers who establish a homestead in California, only to be defeated by a drought. The novel is vastly over-plotted with too many events, both naturalistic and mystical, realistic and symbolic.

Back to his home territory again, and this time he hit pay dirt. *Tortilla Flat* (1935), the episodic adventures of Danny – who, home from World War One, inherits a house on the outskirts of Monterey, lives with fellow bohemians in a town mainly inhabited by out-of-work Mexicans – sold 26,000 copies in its first year and won the Commonwealth Club Gold Medal for the best novel by a California writer.

After the local colour of *Tortilla Flat* Steinbeck seems to have judged that it was time, once again, for something more ambitious. This turned into *In Dubious Battle* (1936) his attempt to dramatise farm labour unrest in California's Central Valley in the light of his friend Ed Rickets's "Phalanx Theory". The book was generally, if guardedly well received, except by the young Mary McCarthy, who wrote in The Nation that although "a natural story teller", Steinbeck "was certainly no philosopher, sociologist, or strike tactician", and regretted that "the legitimately dramatic incidents of the strike should be subordinated to such infantile verbalizations".

It was time for Steinbeck, once again, to return to more familiar material. The result was *Of Mice and Men*. Now that he and Carol were living comfortably in their new Los Gatos ranch house, Steinbeck settled down to a happy period of regular composition.

Up to this point Steinbeck's literary output had alternated between literary or intellectual experiments and more realistic work based on people and landscapes more familiar to him. Then came *The Grapes of Wrath*, which was both ambitious in its epic scale and based on his experience of finally meeting migrant farm workers face to face in order to write a series of newspaper articles about their predicament. With this synthesis of realistic characters and events based on the author's experience, and the ambition of the author's imaginative recreation of a whole movement in American history, *The Grapes of Wrath* (1939) was John Steinbeck's masterpiece, and the work for which he is still best known today.

A SHORT CHRONOLOGY

1902 February 27 John Ernst Steinbeck, Jr. born in Salinas, California.

1920 The US constition is amended to give women in all states the right to vote.

1927 October 29 The Wall Street Crash (also known as Black Tuesday) – the beginning of the Great Depression.

1933 Introduction of the New Deal, a series of initiatives to stimulate the economy and help victims of the depression.

1934 The first of three severe droughts in the US prairies, leading to the agriculturally devastating 'Dust Bowl' of the 1930s.

1937 *Of Mice and Men* published.

1939 *The Grapes of Wrath*.

1962 Steinbeck wins the Nobel Prize for literature.

1939 *East of Eden*.

1968 December 20 Steinbeck dies in New York.

FURTHER READING

There are two biographies of Steinbeck in the frame, both worth reading or consulting. The more substantial is Jackson Benson's *The True Adventures of John Steinbeck, Writer*. (London: Heinemann, 1984), but Jay Parini's *John Steinbeck: A Biography* (New York: Henry Holt, 1995) is well written and full of illuminating detail.

Steinbeck was a prolific and revealing letter writer, and references to *Steinbeck: A Life in Letters*, edited by Elaine Steinbeck and Robert Wallsten (London: Heinemann, 1975) should accompany readings in the author's biography.

As for criticism, one could start with the selection edited by Donald R. Noble, *The Steinbeck Question: New Essays in Criticism* (Troy, NY: Whitston, 1993) and John Ditsky's *John Steinbeck and the Critics*. Rochester: Camden House, 2000). For a feminist view, see Cynthia Burkhead's *Student Companion to John Steinbeck* (Westport, Conn.: Greenwood Press, 2002).

For criticism on *Of Mice and Men* specifically, have a look at the essays pertaining to the novel in Jackson Benson's useful collection *The Short Novels of John Steinbeck: Critical Essays with a Checklist Of Mice and Men* (Durham: Duke University Press, 1990).

Immediate reactions to the novel can be found in *John Steinbeck: The Contemporary Reviews*, edited by Joseph P. McElrath, Jr., Jesse S. Crisler and Susan Shillinglaw (Cambridge: Cambridge University Press, 1996).

But the most rewarding and productive further reading would be in other books by Steinbeck himself. Students wanting a fuller understanding of the author's work should read at least *Tortilla Flat* (1935) and *The Grapes of Wrath* (1939). Later novels worth knowing are *The Pearl* (1947) and *East of Eden* (1952), which he considered his great work. To get an idea of how good his documentary journalism was, see *A Russian Journal* (1948), the book he did with the Magnum photographer Robert Capa, following their visit to the Soviet Union, and the compilation of his World War II dispatches, *Once There Was a War* (1958).

Notes

ALSO AVAILABLE

Connell Short Guides
A Doll's House
A Room with a View
A Streetcar Named Desire
An Inspector Calls
Animal Farm
Atonement
Beloved
Birdsong
Never Let Me Go
Rebecca
Spies
The Bloody Chamber
The Catcher in the Rye
The History Boys
The Road
Waiting for Godot

Connell Guides
Emma
Far From the Madding Crowd
Frankenstein
Great Expectations
Hard Times
Heart of Darkness
Jane Eyre
Lord of the Flies

Mansfield Park
Middlemarch
Mrs Dalloway
Paradise Lost
Persuasion
Pride and Prejudice
Tess of the D'Urbervilles
The Canterbury Tales
The Great Gatsby
The Poetry of Robert Browning
The Waste Land
To Kill A Mockingbird
Wuthering Heights

Shakespeare Guides
A Midsummer Night's Dream
Antony and Cleopatra
Hamlet
Julius Caesar
King Lear
Macbeth
Othello
Romeo and Juliet
Second Tetralogy
The Tempest
Twelfth Night

To order any of our guides, and for more information on forthcoming titles, please visit our website:

www.connellguides.com

First published in 2016 by
Connell Guides
Artist House
35 Little Russell Street
London WC1A 2HH

10 9 8 7 6 5 4 3 2 1

Picture credits:
p.3 © Library of Congress
p.24 © Alamy

A CIP catalogue record for this book is available from the British Library.
ISBN 978-1-911187-06-6

Design © Nathan Burton
Assistant Editors:
Brian Scrivener & Paul Woodward

Printed by Short Run Press Ltd, Exeter

www.connellguides.com